*The Owner's Manual for the
Dental Team Member*

YOUR KEY TO THE PRACTICE

12 Easy Steps to Greater Emotional & Financial Security

by Linda Miles & Walter Hailey

with illustrations by Dr. Phil Korpi, the cartoon dentist

Triamid Press
Chicago • Dallas

This book is a gift from:

This book belongs to:

ISBN 1-882306-06-6
Library of Congress Catalog Card Number : 95-61624

Triamid Press
Chicago • Dallas

Acknowledgments

I would like to thank the entire dental industry for their support and feedback over the past 17 years. We have consulted in over 1,000 dental practices and lectured to more than 40,000 people annually over the past ten years. Their requests and revelations of their relationships made this content possible. I would like to thank my husband, Don, for his encouragement and understanding when commitments and projects interrupted many of our days and weekends. I would also like to thank my staff who share my enthusiasm, client service and dedication to each task (speaking, consulting, writing, product development). Last, but certainly not least, I would like to thank Walter Hailey, Steve Anderson, Kirpal Gordon and the entire staff of Planned Marketing Associates. Spending time with them at "The Ranch", Padre Island and in Virginia Beach to write this book has been one of the most rewarding experiences of my career.

Linda L. Miles

The best ideas have always come from linking up basic truths in a unique way. The ideas for this book have been no different and came from special people who really care about dentistry and the people in it. This book owes its beginning to Ruth Port in Sydney, Australia, whose wisdom linked up Linda and I for the first time. Without the support and encouragement of our many Dental Boot Kamp graduates, this book would never have been conceived. Thanks to Dr. McHenry "Mac" Lee and Joleen Jackson, who helped launch and oversee the dental division of Planned Marketing, and who continually work to make the proven business systems we teach practical to implement in the dental office. Thanks to Kirpal Gordon for making all of our ideas work on paper and being the Hailey-Miles bridge. A special thanks to Steve Anderson who has as much faith in me as I have in him. I especially would like to thank Don and Linda Miles, who were such a delight to work with. Above all, I would like to thank my wife, Barbara, who has been a true partner and support in all of our travels and in opening her heart and her home to dentists from around the world.

We are fortunate to have a great number of dental mentors, some of whom we have listed in the back of this book, whose influence has changed our lives.

Walter Hailey

Preface

For twenty years Linda Miles has consulted with thousands of dental practices throughout the United States, Canada and Australia. Her tapes and seminars on office management are well known throughout the international dental community. A strong believer in the team member approach, she is regarded as the foremost in her field.

Walter Hailey of Planned Marketing Associates has spent over forty years building businesses. His dental "Boot Kamps" are providing dentists and their teams with innovative perspectives in marketing and the people skill side of dentistry.

Are their ideas effective? Consider these comments.

For Linda Miles:

•*Since we started with Linda Miles's consulting services we've achieved results that we didn't know were possible. Our hygienists and assistants are presenting so much dentistry to our new patients and recare patients that we're now booked way in advance. Our production has doubled in the first year after the consult, and we are reaching our second year production goals. It's a pleasure to be doing quality dentistry without compromise.*

——-Denny Mills, D.D.S., Deadwood SD

•*Our in-office consultation with Linda Miles has given our staff not only a new direction but a new sense of cooperation allowing us to move forward to new levels of productivity and profit as a cohesive team.*

—Dr. David Roshkind, West Palm Beach FL

•*Linda Miles has made the largest impact and most significant improvement to my professional life.*

—-Larry Streleck, D.D.S., Rapid City SD

•*Every dental practice needs the challenge Linda Miles presents. Her seminars demonstrate the value of good planning, good communication and good work.*

—-Dr. Richard Cooper, West Palm Beach FL

•*Linda's impact on my practice has been incredible. My father taught me the fine art of clinical dentistry, but Linda taught me the fine art of dentistry as a business!*

—-Dr. Philip Carson, Chattanooga TN

•*The Linda Miles seminar on office management was "just what the doctor ordered." It was the best two days of my life!* —-Dr. Penny Wood, Crestview FL

•*Linda Miles's management advice has been responsible for an enormous increase in productivity, profitability and staff enthusiasm. My dental team always accepts her suggestions because they know how much Linda values their importance to the practice.* —-Dr. Charles Wood, Alburquerque NM

•*I began working with Miles & Associates six years ago, attending seminars and studying the tape series. But her office consultation has proven to be the most beneficial of all. The telephone follow-up service is excellent for intermittent problem solving. The growth I attribute to Ms Miles is a fantastic and cohesive staff, greatly reduced stress and a gross that has tripled.* —-Dr. Joel Safer, Baton Rouge LA

•The value of Linda's seminar is that she taught my staff and I how to make a great work environment in which we all can grow together. —John Burgess, D.D.S., Charleston WV

And for Walter Hailey:

•Walter Hailey's concepts and philosophies have impacted my life beyond description. Of all the implementations we have used in our office over the years, this is without a doubt the most powerful. —Marcos Ortega, D.D.S., San Diego CA

•There are probably hundreds of ways in which my staff and I have been helped by Walter Hailey, but the material on self-esteem has changed the way we talk to one another, do business, even see the world around us. Increasing profits by $200,000 is only one result. Every day I see Walter's wisdom at work. —Alan Goldstein, D.M.D., P.C., New York NY

•Prior to coming I was sick and tired of being sick and tired. I no longer controlled my practice; my practice controlled me. Hailey understood what I needed. I now look forward to starting the day instead of dreading it. The month immediately following the "Boot Kamp," our team produced more than in any other month in my fourteen years of practicing dentistry! —Dr. Thomas Volck, Vandalia OH

•We're not sure if we're more excited by the great increase in patient acceptance of treatment or the fact that we've actually been empowered to come back and LEAD our staff. We're functioning like professionals who have given up their approval addiction and are taking charge—-without a consultant standing over us! The changes in our staff already have paid enormous dividends. Your care, effort, motivation and wisdom are indeed a blessing. We now know why you're called the "YES" company.
—Linda Walters, D.M.D, and Robert Ferguson, D.M.D., Winter Park, FL

•The communication techniques my dental team and I learned at the "Boot Kamp" have turned our practice around. The bottom line is that our gross production will exceed $500,000 this year compared to $380,000 last year. Not bad for a practice that sees patients only three days a week.
                    —James Moore, D.D.S., Bridgeton, MO

•Like Walter says, the key is to align yourself with the proper whos, and the people at Planned Marketing Associates are some of the finest, most dedicated professionals I've ever had the pleasure to learn from. Walter created the most meaningful learning experience of my nineteen year dental hygiene career.
                    —Janice Schwartz, R.D.H., Middlesex NJ

•Keep doing what you are doing! After using the principles and techniques we learned at your dental "Boot Kamp," we realized an additional 15% increase in profitability, which puts our practice in the $750,000 production category.
                    —William Locante, D.D.S., Memphis TN

•I am continually struck by how aptly your program is named. My military boot camp experience was far less pleasant, but certainly no more life changing than what happened to me in Hunt, Texas. The skills I learned have obvious extension out of the office and into my life. Hailey does a terrific job at helping those who need courage to change and improve their lives.
                    —Dr. A. Keith Phillips, Winston-Salem NC

•The power of the "Boot Kamp" continues to astound me. The sections on planning and prioritizing were particularly enlightening. I am "life enriched." My relationship with patients and with my dental team has changed dramatically. You've helped me bring focus to myself and my work.
                    —Robin Steely, D.D.S., Battle Creek MI

Because they come from two different yet complimentary perspectives, Linda and Walter were asked to share ideas to help teams and individuals be more effective. The following pages are the result of that collaboration.

But be forewarned: If books are written merely to be read, then this is not a book. It was written to encourage you to act! Its purpose is to help you develop—and own—the twelve qualities most crucial for career success in the dental office.

The pages between these covers are yours. Have your pen ready to write in them. Make notes to yourself in the margins. Answer the questions and complete the Personal Action Plan at the end of each chapter.

Make it *your* plan of action.

The key purpose of all education is not knowledge but ACTION.

Introduction

When you chose to work in the dental profession, you chose one of the most lucrative careers in the world.

Proportional to the level of education necessary to the job, each member of a dental team enjoys better pay, better benefits, better hours and better opportunity for growth than almost any other occupation.

Why? The revolution in technology and the birth of the Information Age have been very good to dentistry. Thirty years ago everyone assumed one in two adult patients would lose their teeth. But the preventative, restorative and cosmetic dentistry of today has changed all that. What was once guesswork in diagnosis and treatment is now an art and science.

And who is the market for these services?

The 80 million Baby Boomers, the wealthiest generation in history, who are at the peak of their earning power for the next fifteen to twenty years.

Their motivation is to look good and feel good. And they are willing to pay whatever price they have to in order to get it. Furthermore, unlike every other professional in this country, dental practices don't compete against each other. *They compete in an untapped market.* Last year alone, an estimated thirty-one billion dollars of necessary dentistry was not performed. In addition, half of the American population has no permanent, happy dental home. Now is the time to take advantage of this window of opportunity. The chance to develop and expand a successful dental practice is unprecedented.

No dental practice can expect to achieve optimum results without a committed team capable of responding to the changes in the market.

Those team members who can work together and who can add value to the practice will have the most stable career with maximum emotional and financial security. The days of "It's not my fault" and "I didn't do it" and "Don't ask me to think" are over. Rather than ride the coattails of the dentist, the team member who is adaptable, willing to learn and self-motivated is the kind of individual that practices increasingly require and reward.

The work habits of the world are undergoing drastic changes and for those who understand that they are the architects of their own careers, the field of dentistry offers the greatest possible opportunities. Though you are employed by a dental practice, it may be more appropriate to recognize **you're in business for yourself.**

Employer/employee loyalty is one tenth what it was twenty years ago. Employees must continue to make themselves employable in today's marketplace. Employees must invest their own time, money and energy into long term career building.

These twelve ground rules for success in the dental office are written as prescriptions-in-a-capsule. Arranged for instant reference, each chapter is not only a reminder all its own, but it builds on principles we feel to be central to greater job satisfaction.

We hope you'll open these pages regularly, use them as a handbook, think seriously about the ideas they contain and see their application in other areas of your life as well. Our years of building business and consulting with dental practices confirm what is at the heart of each of these chapters:

The only real career security is in helping provide the practice with happy, paying patients who pay more than it costs to get them.

Chapter 1

**"Since you're new here, I want to warn you about
gossip in the office – I mean let me tell you what I
heard the assistant say about the hygienist!"**

Gossip

Imagine the following scenario.

Helen Hush-hush is in her second week as the new hygienist. She has worked in many dental offices before, and at times she has thought that people just didn't like her. However, in her new job she has become fast friends with the appointment coordinator, Danielle Dropjaw. The scene opens, from the point of view of a patient in the reception area.

"Do you know what I heard yesterday, Danielle?"

"No, tell me, tell me."

"Doctor Difficult said that he didn't like the way you answered the phone. Can you believe that?"

"Who was he talking to?"

"To Karen. He told her that she was the best chairside assistant he had ever had."

"But I've been with him for ten years. Karen's only been here six months!"

"Well, what can I tell you? I think he was mad at me also for botching a number of procedures. I guess the only kind of help that he likes is the kind that thinks he's God's gift to the world!"

Sound familiar?

The causes of gossip go deep as human weakness itself. Self-doubt, jealousy, personal insecurity, the fear of communicating directly, the perception of favoritism—-these motivate gossip. Putting others down in an attempt to make oneself look good is not the behavior of a person with a high degree of self esteem or empathy for others.

Don't think for a moment that such thoughtless chatter doesn't damage a practice environment. A mood of mistrust and a sense of turmoil hangs in the air. Gossip has the unfortunate quality of being contagious. Even well adjusted people will gossip, or sub-group, if they sense that they are not getting a fair shake. When the practice administrator or dentist shows favoritism to one or or two team members at the expense of others, the ones left out will counter-attack. This only makes the gossip grapevine grow while making it harder to detect since the gossip perpetrated by the rejected members doesn't feel like sabotage but only getting even.

Linda Miles

Prescription #1

The funny thing about gossip is what it reveals about the needs of each person on the team. The practice of **giving sincere compliments** ends up reversing the tendency to talk about people behind their backs.

Result: Praising others has the effect of also improving one's own "self-esteem meter." Secure people tolerate weakness in others but notice and respond to their strengths. Insecure people are exactly the opposite.

Prescription #2

Establish open communication in team meetings. Set personal goals for every member of the team. Both dentist and team members give a three to five minute report on their goal progress, behaviors they are trying to improve for the sake of the overall success of the practice. Let them ask for help and feedback on ways to improve.

Result: Such a "health of the practice and my role in making it better" report allows others to see your commitment to the practice, thereby reinforcing the idea that each member of the team has an integral part to play in improving performance. It also lessens the suspicion factor that helps gossip thrive. Finally, it humanizes individuals, allowing others to see them as working on themselves for the betterment of all.

Walter Hailey
Prescription #3
Like that famous Argentine dance, it takes two to gossip, the person talking and the person listening. **Not getting caught in the gossip mill** is the beginning of the solution.
"Hey, do you know what Doctor Difficult said about me?"
"Well, have you talked to him about it?"
"No."
"So let's go find him. You two need to talk."
Result: If you refuse to be a receiver of gossip and if you furthermore **take it back to the source**, you have:
a) solved the problem. Knowing your integrity is high, they
b) won't waste your time with gossip. Instead, they
c) know they can build trust with you.
Individuals have values as varied as birds. When your values reach beyond the little squabbles that weaken the effectiveness of the dental team, we call you an eagle.
Let's return to the original scenario.
Helen did one thing wrong with two results. She undermined the dentist's credibility to a fellow team member, which already makes her a turkey. But she failed to consider the stunned patient who overheard her from the reception area. However accidentally, she betrayed the patient's confidence in the dentist and the entire practice.
An eagle flies high enough to see that the purpose of the practice is the health and well being of the patient. The resourceful team member understands that earning the patient's confidence is the duty of the entire dental team, not just the dentist. The practice of earning that confidence becomes as contagious as gossip.
The difference is in the results.

the gossip / trust chart

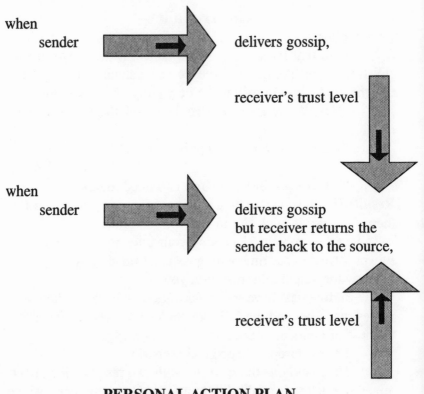

when
  sender   delivers gossip,

receiver's trust level

when
  sender   delivers gossip
                but receiver returns the
                sender back to the source,

receiver's trust level

PERSONAL ACTION PLAN

1. List the names of every person on your dental team (if the team is small, fill in with suppliers or vendors). Next to the name write the three most valuable characteristics they bring to the practice:

Name   *Positive Characteristics*

_____   _____

_____   _____

_____   _____

Send a message. Within two working days, let each person on board know the positive characteristics you see in them. Make a habit of not letting a day pass without a positive remark to a team member. Don't forget: **if someone else overhears you making a compliment, that's all for the better!** It's one sure way to build harmony within the team. If patients overhear these positive compliments, their trust level in the practice is strengthened.

2. Set personal goals for yourself. List below the behaviors you want to improve upon for the sake of the dental practice:

_____

_____

_____

_____

At the next weekly meeting or team huddle, announce this list of goals. Invite the other members of the team to comment. **Encourage their feedback.**
Promise them that you will consider all suggestions. Report on your progress regularly.

3. Imagine that you are approached by someone in the office who has a problem with a another team member. Recall the gossip/trust chart. Instead of getting "sucked in" to the gossip game, picture yourself with the integrity to send the person back to the source to solve the problem. Write down what you will say if you should be approached:

_____

_____

_____

4. What else can you do to stop gossip?

Chapter 2

"I'll call you back later, O.K.?
I can't concentrate anyway – there's
a patient here interrupting me!"

Checking Personal Baggage at the Door

We've all been to department stores where the sales clerk just couldn't be bothered. Yakking on the phone, chatting it up with the other employees, refusing to recognize customers, the clerk gives the impression that the last thing on his or her mind is the job.

Ignored, dismissed and forgotten, we either find the item ourselves, get someone else's help or leave the store. What is management thinking, we ask ourselves, putting such a discourteous sales staff on the floor?

The answer is probably that they aren't thinking at all.

Compare this scenario with a well-run dental office. All members of the team are on the same page. Though they may enjoy conversing on the phone or with each other, the dental team immediately recognizes the patient when he or she arrives. Courtesy and concern are the standards the team sets. Instead of feeling ignored, the patient feels cared for and listened to totally. After all, it's the dental health of the patient that is the central reason everyone is there in the first place.

How does a dental team learn to "check personal baggage at the door?"

Walter

Prescription #1

When you go to work, you're on stage.

The audience is the patient, and your focus is on creating a climate where the patient can relax. Roger Cameron and Rene Brooks, recruiters for Fortune 500 companies, have a proven exercise they use.

They recommend, on your way to work, that you mark a familiar sight, whether it's a tree by your home or the line separating the office from the rest of the world. At this marker, **leave all personal problems behind you.** From that moment on until you re-claim your "belongings" at the end of the day, your mind is now free to focus with a laser-like beam on other people first. This goes beyond the description for appointment coordinator, financial coordinator, practice administrator, hygienist, assistant or dentist.

It means that you make sure that patients like themselves better when they are in the dental office.
Result: Patients RETURN and REFER other patients because they like the way they feel in your care.

Prescription #2
We feel this is so important that we have an additional exercise. Whatever is holding up that laser-like focus, whether it's the mortgage or Junior's note from school or a change in the weather, write it down.

We call it **a junk sheet.** When you've listed all those things that might compromise your mental commitment, crumple up the sheet and throw the junk away.
Result: We guarantee your attention will become as focused as a puppy's when its master has hamburger meat in his hand.

But what about those behaviors which we don't realize may negatively impact upon the patient's sense of well being?

Linda
Prescription #3
Some people are just not "tuned in." It may never occur to certain individuals that having a conversation with another team member about personal business in front of the patient is wrong. It's another form of ignoring the patient.

This lack of recognition extends to many "office privileges." In our experience consulting with dental practices that have problems, too often it isn't until "privileges" have been abused that the dental team begins to set limits about things like personal calls, lateness or absence.

But for the truly motivated team member, waiting for things to go wrong or for a policy to be invented is simply unacceptable.

Set your own standard.

It's as simple as asking yourself, "What kind of office would this be if everyone in it were to act just like me?"

Result: This is the greatest safeguard against taking something a little too much for granted.

Do misperceived "privileges" extend beyond tardiness or having a personal conversation with a co-worker while a patient is present?

Linda

Prescription #4

Let's discuss dentist and team member relations. As in the prescription for abusing office privileges, the intent to injure or destroy need not be present for real trouble to appear all the same. Because perception IS reality, the safest thing to do is to prevent even the appearance of impropriety in all dealings with the dentist.

Do not attempt to have the dentist solve your personal problems. Do not seek to meet the dentist after hours or on the doctor's personal lunch break.

Though he or she may be concerned, comforting and even willing to lend support, the dentist/employer is a bad choice for a personal confidante! The male employer who offers assistance to female employees in their personal problems becomes a target for other serious practice problems.

Familiarity of this kind can breed more than just contempt. It can lead to the destruction of family units, disgrace and bankruptcy as well as sexual harassment charges and embezzlement.

The dentist's reputation, as well as your own, is crucial to the patients as well as everyone else on team and their families. It's important to recognize that desperate people in desperate situations do desperate things. They will read many fantasies into a smile or your meeting the dentist after hours. Jealousy, the perception of favoritism, a sense of having been wronged—all can become a license to steal. And with the threat of sexual misconduct exposed, even if everything is actually above board, blowing the whistle is a good deal more difficult.

But let's face it: we're human; we all have problems in our personal lives and the dentist/employer often appears a tower of strength. This is why the best prescription of all is to **ask the dentist for a professional they could recommend.**

A marriage counselor, a financial advisor, a therapist, a member of the clergy—the dentist is likely to know someone who can help.

Result: Such a request makes it clear that you respect the dentist's judgment. It lets the dentist know what you're going through without the burden of obligation or the suggestion of innuendo. Furthermore, people who love to talk will have no ammunition.

Walter

Prescription #5

Because hanky panky between a team member and the dentist has ruined a great many practices, a word of caution about "office affairs" is in order. Common sense ought to tell us that such a situation is unwise for all concerned. But this is an area where even marriage vows, let alone common sense, sometimes mean very little.

Here's what I tell my grandchildren: even when both parties are single and available, it's no easy ride. The dual roles of being an effective dental team member AND a sexual love partner to the dentist can easily come into conflict. Not only does the dance of courtship now have to step over the booby traps of the office and the possibility of lowering team morale, but what chance does the team member really have? Talk about putting all of your eggs in one basket—-if the romance dies, so does the likelihood of your employment! The heart, as Shakespeare wrote, may have reasons that reason knows nothing of, but the fear of losing your job can sober you up from even the most intoxicating passion.

I'm no preacher and I've no sermons, but if it's real love, ask the dentist for a recommendation to work in another office. **Result:** This way both the relationship and the dental team are respected and not compromised.

PERSONAL ACTION PLAN

1. Fill in the diagram below.

Write down the spot that you pass daily on your way to work that you will now use as the line to remind you to leave all personal problems behind and focus like a laser beam on the task at hand:

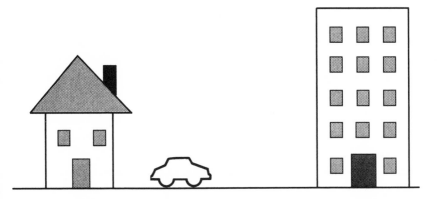

2. Review the prescription for giving your mind the freedom to think about the other person first instead of yourself when you're at work. Fill in as quickly as you can.

JUNK

Write it down. . .

_____

_____

_____

_____

_____

_____

_____

_____

_____

_____

_____

_____

_____

. . . now chunk the junk

3. List the standards that you set for your own personal behavior in the office. Review the prescription against abusing office privileges and write those personal standards in underneath the Olympic torch:

4. What proven mentors, family members and experienced counselors can I go to help me address personal problems:

_____

_____

_____

5. How can I avoid the appearance of evil and help protect the reputation of the dentist and the entire team?

_____

_____

_____

Chapter 3

"I know you're a busy man, Doctor, but I wanted to bring
you my list of problems in the office before the hygienist
and the office administrator brought you theirs!"

Being a Fixer, Not a Finger Pointer

One of the major differences between the successful dental office and the struggling one is the way in which unforeseen emergencies are resolved.

As we all know, "stuff" happens. Supplies we ordered never arrive, bridges come back from the laboratory with the wrong specifications, the compressor breaks, the computer goes down, Mrs. Jones never stops calling about her crown, patients complain about a lack of parking—the problem is not the length of the list but how we perceive the problem itself.

Walter

Prescription #1

In every adversity is hidden the seed of an equal or greater opportunity.

Like a mystery novel in which the detective mulls over clues, every problem seeks to be matched up with a satisfying solution. Get into the spirit of the investigation. If there's a formula at all, it has more to do with developing trust between team member and dentist than with having the answer before the question can be asked.

Creating permission to share sound ideas is the first prerequisite. Approach the dentist with possible options rather than with dread and terror. "Help, doctor, quick, please," are not the first four words you want to say.

If you identify a problem, be sure to offer at least two or three possible solutions, one of which is inexpensive. Remember that, according to the degree of emergency, there are long term and short term solutions.

Become known as a creative problem solver.

Develop the reputation for being the source of good ideas. Realize that the quality of those ideas goes up the more you work at it. The ultimate point to be reached is where you don't need to ask the dentist about every little detail or concern. **Result:** The dentist discovers that you can be depended upon to think clearly and in the interests of the practice. In turn, you get to know what the dentist is comfortable with and an atmosphere of mutual respect develops. **Putting your heads together becomes synergy.**

Trust is the bond and the bridge.

Fingers isolate; hands build!

How do we create the conditions that maximize and build trust?

Linda

Prescription #2

Make sure that if someone brings you a problem you will see it through to its resolution. To **create closure on a task**—-seeing to it personally that the problem ends up resolved—-proves that you care. You can be relied upon to help fix the problem, not just point it out in panic.

Compare this approach to "It's not my fault" or the it's-not-my-job syndrome which sends a message that you really can't be bothered to think at all. **Blame laying and guilty consciences have no place in a professional setting.** Particularly when everyone is busy, the best thing to do is not add to the confusion by making excuses.

Handling the error with quiet skill will deliver the impression you're actually looking to create.

Result: Since you're able to respond, the dentist and everyone on the team will see you as responsible, resourceful and capable.

Is it possible to assume too much responsibility?

Walter

Prescription #3

People reward action. Keeping the patient happy and getting the problem taken care of is the balance you should seek to achieve. But charging ahead with your own solutions without having any authority to do so will cause more problems than you will solve.

Being neither owner nor employer, you must remember you're not just representing yourself but the dentist and the entire practice. Trust is developed over time.

The fastest way to develop the owner's trust is to be trustworthy! Think the way the owner would think.

And how does trust grow?

Trust begins with the permission to share smart ideas. Trust becomes strengthened by the quality and implementation of those ideas.

Confidence comes when you know that you and the dentist, you and the practice, you and the rest of the dental team are working together. That confidence becomes contagious. Then, when those unforeseen emergencies take place, they become an intriguing puzzle to solve. Just like the pleasure a good mystery gives, the problems excite your imagination rather than fill you with fear and panic.

The additional benefit of earning the reputation for being a problem solver is that you truly become an indispensable asset to your team.

PERSONAL ACTION PLAN

1. What are the major challenges in our practice that are presently unresolved:

_____

_____

_____

_____

_____

_____

2. What are three possible solutions to each of these challenges?

_____

_____

_____

_____

_____

_____

3. What can you do in the future to take care of a problem when it arises rather than dumping it on someone else or simply avoiding it?

_____

_____

_____

Chapter 4

"Oh, that! We couldn't decide whose job
description it was to clean the refrigerator in the
staff lounge, so we just sealed it permanently!"

Assuming Roles

Imagine an ideal work environment.

Not only do you know what's going on, you can see how all are working together to realize a common goal. You know what you're doing there, what's expected of you, what should and shouldn't happen. Things are clear.

Behind such a picture are two necessary and important constants. The first is leadership—-strong, dependable and steady; the second is that the tasks that must be done are clearly defined so everyone knows their role in the proper order of things.

In the real world, gaps between job descriptions are inevitable. As nature abhors a vacuum, those gaps must get filled in. Whether it's as mundane as who turns the lights off or as crucial as who makes sure that you get paid, the question we must ask ourselves is: which roles are mine?

Among the most enlightened dental teams, composed of players who are not simply going to a job but who are managing their own careers, these gaps still happen but they do not set the entire team in chaos. Because each member of the team is his or her *own leader,* who will assume what role does not carry with it the degree of jealousy, squabbling, and unhappiness which sometimes rule the less harmonious dental office where leadership is unclear.

In other words the two errors that the team makes in this regard—-becoming the office witch or becoming the office wimp—-can be avoided.
These two extremes tend to create each other. When team members cop out and get wimpy in the face of what needs to get done, a "leader" emerges who has no real power, commands no real respect and knows little more than anyone else. This new dictator can turn the mood of the office into one of suspicion and in-fighting.

The problem stems from not knowing what one ought to do. How can one guard against such a wrong turn?

How can we learn which roles are our own?

Walter

Bum Phillips, former coach of the Houston Oilers, likes to say there were only two types of players he couldn't work with: the player who would NOT DO ANYTHING he asked him to do and the player who would ONLY DO what he asked him to do.

The best way to fill the vacuum between job descriptions is a three phase approach:

Phase 1
Manage your own position first. If you don't know what should be done, ASK. Don't wait to be told. By then it's already too late.
If in doubt, find out.
You do that by asking: **what outcomes does the dentist perceive me responsible for?** Notice the key word is not what jobs, but what outcomes. From childhood to senility, we're much more comfortable when we know what is expected of us. Once the doctor has written down the expectations of

your job description—-daily, weekly, monthly, quarterly and annually—-you know what should be done.
Result: You become accountable.

Phase 2

The next question you must ask yourself is: **what guidelines do I have to achieve these outcomes?** You need to know all the dos and don'ts. If I'm accountable for a clean treatment room, I need to know that the office policy is not to clean up while a patient is in the chair. If I'm responsible for collections, I need to know that after 45 days it's time to ask for that money.
Result: You become acquainted with all the resources you need to get the job done properly.

Phase #3

There's one more question to ask: **how will the dentist measure success or failure on performing this task?**
Tied to the notion of expectations is the need for inspections. The worst way to run a business is to have a lot to expect but nothing to inspect.
Result: People perform tasks better when the results of that performance are inspected. Knowing this makes all the difference in the world!

What if the dentist does not inspect your work?

Phase #4

Create your own inspection!
As all the prescriptions in this booklet are essentially self administrating, so too with inspections.
Let me offer an example that Steve Anderson, President of Planned Marketing Associates, tells about **the power of taking personal responsibility for your job**. A client of ours was Director for Human Resources for a major insurance company in Texas. After he had gone to one of our "Boot Kamps," he approached the head of the firm and asked, "What can I do to make myself more valuable?"

Surprised and pleased, the head of the company said, "Let me think." The following week our client was promoted to the executive committee.

Result: He did two things right: he cared and he asked.

It may seem noble to hide your light under the proverbial bushel basket, but it will keep you in the dark at promotion time.

MAKE SURE ALL TASKS, EVEN THOSE NOT ENCLOSED WITHIN JOB BOUNDARIES, GET TAKEN CARE OF.

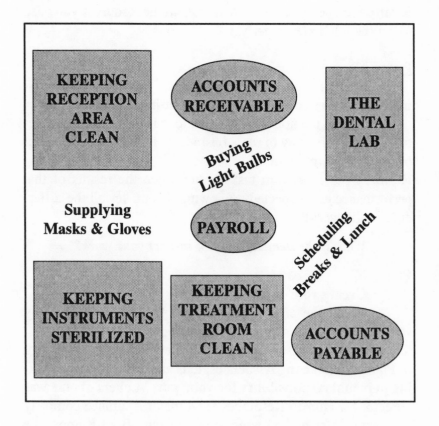

Don't let "the little things" slip through the cracks.

PERSONAL ACTION PLAN

1. List all the outcomes you are responsible for in the practice:

_____

_____

_____

_____

_____

2. List the guidelines you have to achieve those outcomes:

_____

_____

_____

_____

_____

3. How is your success measured?

_____

_____

_____

4. When will you ask the dentist, "What can I do to make myself more valuable?"

_____

_____

Chapter 5

"Some people think the doctor is merely a 'yes man'
to his wife in this practice, but that just isn't true –
when she says 'no', he says 'no', too!"

Dealing with the Spouse of the Dentist

In addition to the ideal work environment described at the beginning of Chapter 4, consider now the ideal role the spouse of the dentist plays in the practice. One team member described her this way: "She's the glue that holds the office together. She's a gem of a co-worker, but she also goes to bat for the team when the dentist isn't supporting our ideas."

How can you help make the spouse of the dentist a key, supportive member of your team?

Linda

Prescription #1

Your job as a member of the dental team is to **support the personal and professional relationship of the dentist and his or her spouse.** Under stress, this can be difficult to remember to do. Consider these reminders:

•It is never a mistake to treat the spouse as the co-owner of the practice;

•Praise the dentist in his or her absence to the spouse; likewise, compliment the spouse in his or her absence to the dentist;

•A good marriage is a union of complimenting energies. Differences in management style ought to be expected rather than regretted;

•Never become a receptacle for the airing of personal

differences between the dentist and the spouse.

Result: Free from having to take sides, you have the opportunity to appreciate the gifts both the husband and wife bring to the practice.

What if there is confusion about the part that the spouse plays in the practice?

Prescription #2

As Walter said in the previous chapter, the first responsibility of a team member is to know what roles you have for the overall effectiveness of the whole team.

Maintain your station.

Don't get worried over what you cannot control or what someone else may or may not be doing.

Result: By setting an example of excellence you help inspire clarity.

What practical steps can the team take to enhance the spouse's role in the practice?

Prescription #3

A) If you're on the team before the spouse comes on board, **offer assistance in the learning process** just as you would to any new employee going through orientation. Being a mentor can help make the spouse's entrance into the practice as smooth as possible.

B) If the spouse is on the team first, accept the fact that **you are working for a husband and wife team**. Realize they are normally opposite in behavioral and management styles.

C) **Avoid playing one employer against the other**. Ask them who will assume the role of personnel director—-your immediate supervisor—-and what your duties are, based on their individual expectations.

D) **Separate friendship and professional relationships**. Becoming—-or remaining—-the best friend of the dentist's spouse is not a good idea as it plays havoc with office morale and implies favoritism even when there isn't any. If you are best friends with the doctor and/or spouse BEFORE accepting a position in the practice, develop a separate professional relationship at work. And if you meet on the job, keep it professional. Going to lunch with the dentist's spouse or socializing after work can easily become misconstrued as apple polishing for special privileges. **Result:** You become instrumental in creating the most important ingredient in the entire recipe. **Respect is the real basis for any relationship, personal or professional.**

PERSONAL ACTION PLAN

1. What specific things can you do to support the dentist and spouse as a couple and as co-owners of the practice:

_____

_____

2. What can you do to set an example of excellence that will inspire everyone on board to fulfill their roles in the practice:

_____

_____

3. **To get respect, you have to give respect.** What can you do to demonstrate respect for the spouse and maximize the harmony within the entire team:

_____

_____

4. What else can you do to support the dentist's spouse in his or her role whether he/she works in the practice or not?

_____

Chapter 6

KORPI

"Thank you for your great ideas in the staff
meeting today, Doctor. The rest of the team and
I have organized a 'to-do' list for you to review,
and we're excited to see the results!"

Taking the Pressure Off the Dentist

What's it like to be a dentist?

A never-ending learning experience.

Dental school may have prepared your dentist for clinical expertise, but the rest of what he or she does was not learned in school. How to be an employer, how to market the practice, how to manage the office, how to finance its expansion, how to deal with patients so they are eager to receive full comprehensive dentistry—-most dentists learn these crucial things incompletely while in the midst of juggling many other concerns on the job. As we saw in the prescriptions for being a fixer and not a finger pointer, the dentist may literally be besieged with constant demands on his or her attention.

By law the only two things that a dentist does that no one else can do are diagnosis and treatment.

How many other things consume the dentist's attention that someone else could do as effectively or more effectively? Are there ways that the dental team can take the pressure off the dentist?

Walter

Prescription #1

Always be thinking and doing what's most profitable for the practice. If you're not sure what that is, ask yourself: **Am I doing at this moment the most productive thing that will bring us closer to the goal and purpose of the practice?**

After attending a dental "Boot Kamp" and asking this

question, Joleen Jackson, a practice administrator in Edna, Texas, told us that she began to see her role in the practice differently. Her dentist, an expert clinician, felt he was the only one capable of selling the treatment plan to the patient. But he knew little about buying and selling. Being a mother, a comparative shopper and a good listener, she knew a lot more.

She began to help him simply by **making the dentist look good in front of the patient.** First on the telephone and then when the patient entered the office, she made sure the patient knew how conscientious he was and in what high regard he was held as a professional. By the time the patient sat in the chair and met the dentist, he was already a lot closer to deciding in favor of the full treatment plan.

The dentist's weakness was that he was too nice! He knew how necessary the treatment was, but he spoke a dialect of dental-ese that patients did not fully understand.

Result: By making the dentist look good in front of the patient, everyone gained: the patient approved the needed treatment plan; the dentist's self-confidence grew as well as his confidence in his team; and the team sent a message that they are **capable of adding value to the practice.**

No man—-or woman—-is an island. Helping to **cover the dentist's weakness** allows the dentist to focus on his or her strengths.

Walter

Prescription #2

Making the dentist's load lighter can be tricky business. There's first the need to honor the level of commitment that the dentist has made. Very often, his or her entire life is invested in the practice. Loans, debts and payment schedules can grate on anyone's good nature. It can also produce a dentist who is so micro-managing that he or she is actually wasting time.

One of the strangest cases we've had at "Boot Kamp" was a dentist who was such a "control freak" that he barely ever left the office. He did everything himself, including hygiene; he poured his own models, even ran the team meetings. He stayed late every evening, getting on the computer, paying the bills, doing the accounts, ordering all the supplies, checking on the lab work. He even trimmed all his dies under magnification before sending them to the lab! Though he loved dentistry, it was easy to see why the practice was not making any money. He delegated nothing. When asked why he didn't train anyone to do even the smallest procedure, he said, "I never have any time."

A caring, nurturing bond between dentist and team must first be established. One of the easiest ways to get this going is to **find the things the dentist has to do that he or she doesn't like to do or doesn't do well**. As long as it isn't diagnosis and treatment, the team member can make life so much smoother for the doctor by taking over these tasks.

Result: With the load shared, the dentist relaxes, feels freer, is more likely to delegate than stranglehold. It's no longer a question of the admiral going down with the ship; instead, you've helped let the dentist do what he or she does best: dentistry.

Make sure that everyone is free to work on their most productive activity without distractions.

It will prove to be the smartest way to add value to the practice.

PERSONAL ACTION PLAN

1. What are the two most profitable things the dentist does in your practice:

_____

_____

2. What are the most profitable things that you do for the practice:

_____

3. What are the things that the dentist doesn't like to do that you or the team could be doing instead:

_____

Chapter 7

"I don't think Sally understands the dress code,
Doctor. Her hair dye color and her nose ring
never coordinate with her uniform!"

Image and Appearance

We've all had the experience of being helped by someone whose dress, personal hygiene and vocabulary seemed so inappropriate to the setting that we became uncomfortable. The used car salesman in loud colors, wide lapels and the "Hi, guy" approach or the waitress dressed to the nines waiting to be "discovered by Hollywood"—-at best, these situations are too hilarious to feel too embarrassed about. However, when they happen in a dental office, these miscalculations in professional appearance become detrimental to the goal of the practice. How can we avoid making the wrong statement?

Is there a dress-for-success formula in dentistry?
Is there a right and wrong way to decorate the office?

Linda

Prescription #1

Team members should dress in relation to the ambitions of the practice. We've said for years: **a practice will attract the quality of patient the doctor, team and office dress up to.**

If you want more white collar professional patients, the entire team must project an upscale image. If your client base is more laid back, a less formal office environment and a more relaxed dress code are in order. It would be totally out of place for a rural practice to have a marble, glass and brass reception area; similarly in a practice in a major metropolis, a "down home" image is unsuitable.

In addition, even in the most thoughtful office, **an update is necessary every five to seven years.**

Floor and wall coverings as well as other accessories like lighting and furniture, should be updated in the same way that clinical and business technology gets updated—with a fund contributed to monthly so that office renewal does not break the practice.

Not only should the personal appearance of the dental team be in harmony with the style the office is decorated in but a dress code ought to be established so that everyone has a clear basis for appropriate attire. **This is not to curtail freedom, but to focus the team on the goal.** Team meetings are a good place to discuss appropriate hair styles, choice of language and attire.

A "grooming coach" should be appointed whose authority includes checking everyone out in the morning before the first patient walks in.

Result: Rather than inhibit, these checks and balances make sure everyone is comfortable and united.

Walter

<u>Prescription #2</u>

Some years ago when I was in the insurance business, my sales team brought up the question of a dress code. They were moving all over the country, and they saw any number of different people in different places in a day.

What we strove for was to look as good as we could within the boundaries set by the client. Approaching a green grocer in an apron and tie, our salesperson wore a jacket and tie, for example. **The degree of professionalism we maintained was always in keeping with the client's expectations.**

What we found out is that likes like likes. If you look too different, people get a little suspicious. We all tend to believe, like and trust people who look similar to ourselves.

As for what to wear in the dental office, have no doubt. **People expect a certain look when they walk into a professional practice.** Being conscious of what makes people more comfortable is what determines the manner of speech and appearance you choose. For example, our research revealed that females have 25% more credibility when they wear their hair up. Since every woman who works for us wants to increase her credibility, the change happened by itself.

Result: They "do let their hair down" at the end of the day, but they are more confident when dealing with the public because they have a clearer idea about the public's expectations.

After all, **we're not dressing for ourselves or to impress each other: we're dressing in order to help relax the patient and better sell dentistry.**

PERSONAL ACTION PLAN

1. Look around. Based on what you see in decor and dress in your office, who are you attracting to your practice:

_____

_____

_____

_____

_____

2. How are you fitting in to the goals of the practice? What kind of changes do you need to make in your dress and appearance to fit in more:

_____

_____

_____

Chapter 8

"How good is the doctor? Oh, if I was
forced to, I'd say he was O.K., I guess!"

The Power of Praise

They say praise does wonders for the sense of hearing.

Everyone would like to hear and be heard, to be part of a work environment that enjoys harmony and purpose, the kind of office where people don't have to be told what to do.

When the vision of the practice is clearly defined by the leader, it not only pulls the best out of each member individually, but allows the team to act collectively and effectively.

Psychologists tell us that there are four basic motivations to why we go to work:

- **praise**
- **a sense of challenge**
- **the opportunity for growth**
- **economic reward.**

The highest motivator is the first.

Everyone seeks recognition and praise.

Consequently, the most effective offices are staffed by people who want to excel. In order to get more recognition, they are prepared to accept challenges, to learn more, to develop themselves professionally and to share in the collective rewards, all of which helps the dentist reach the mission of the practice.

It all starts with "a vision of the mission of the practice," a <u>cognition</u> that tell us why we are there:

—<u>Re-cognition</u> comes from the leader and is given to those who contribute and help realize the vision;

—(P)raise is the language we share to help us rise to the reminder that we are mobilized and on a mission;

—Recognition and praise strengthen that sense of solidarity that will carry us into our goal of practicing the most successful dentistry we can;

—Teamwork is the by-product, that feeling that we're all in this together, engaged in something larger than ourselves, for the greater good of all.

Compare this feeling of sharing "a magnificent obsession" with a recent survey on national employment:

- *only one out of every four workers* say they are currently working at their actual potential;
- *two out of four* do not put in any more than the minimum of what's required to hold on to the job;
- *three out of four* say they could be more involved, that they don't work as hard as they used to.

What the survey reveals is an increasing tendency to withhold effort on the job.

Why is this so? Not enough recognition! The leader who fails to reward the team with the gratitude commensurate with their achievement is certainly missing a vital opportunity.

But that's only half the equation.

Walter

Prescription #1
Manage your own morale.

Initiate the praise of others. Don't wait for praise to rain down from above. Those who give praise receive more praise in return.

Result: Considering the projections made by "trend prophets," those team members who manage their own morale will be most likely to remain employed—-and will be the most sought after—-while others are let go.

The good news is that this is an area where each individual can take his or her own lead. It's an "inside job."

What are the signs of low morale in an office and what can the dental team member do about it?

Linda

<u>Prescription #2</u>

There are three distinct indicators I look for:

1. Run / Hide / Fix-the-blame-quick.

"It's not my turn, not my job, not my handwriting." To deny responsibility and to blame others for shortcomings indicates that the fear of a reprimand has turned the team member into a person incapable of getting the job done.

The solution is simple. Like the top team players who progress the fastest like to say, *"If I did it, let me admit it! No one is perfect. Everyone makes mistakes."*

Result: Someone addresses the problem, it gets resolved and the whole team moves closer to the goal.

2. Look at me! / I'm grand! / I've done it again.

Publicly patting yourself on the back too much is an indication of insecurity. It can also take the form of martyrdom. "I know it's your turn to take out the trash but I did it for you." Or, "Doesn't the supply closet look nice, Doctor, I sacrificed my lunch hour organizing it."

Though the team member may feel saintly and close to getting canonized, the behavior can drive everyone else up a wall. The best prescription is to praise others before they feel the need to praise themselves.

Result: Having beaten the team member to the punch, you accentuate the positive behavior before it becomes part of the "No one appreciates what I do around here" complaint.

3. I'm right and you're wrong and that's final.

Some people feel they always have to be right no matter what. If you see this insistence in yourself, recognize it for what it really is: trying to defend a weak position just because it's yours! There's a simple reminder:

Become committed to WHAT is right, not WHO is right.

Result: The defensive behavior, which weakens the pathway to solutions, is replaced by a greater receptivity to the issue at hand.

What is the barometer for how well your team supports and praises one another?

Linda

Prescription #3

That's easy. Take an objective look and see *how the patients are treated*—on the phone, in the office, and in the chair. Listen for how the team discusses the patients in their absence.

How the team treats the patients is the best indication of how the team treats each other.

If the indication is not good, go back and look at how the team is failing to support and encourage each other. The error always begins on the inside and then works its way out.

For the dentist or team member who feels that "if I give compliments the team will expect it out of me and frankly it isn't in my personality to praise or recognize others and it's too exhausting anyway," I offer what years in the field have shown me. I've consulted with both kinds of offices, ones where there is no recognition among the team and ones where the entire dental team jumps through hoops for each other and the patients because praise and incentive are the order of the day.

There just is no comparison.

Result: Behavior that is appreciated is behavior that will be repeated.

Are there other advantages of praise and recognition?

Linda

Prescription #4

There is a ton of power in praising the doctor to the patients.

Become a chairside cheerleader or a telephone town crier. The greatest value you can have is to praise the dentist in his or her absence. This does five things:

- *reassures first time patients;*
- *increases case acceptance;*
- *builds trust with patients;*
- *develops trust from the team;*
- *enhances the doctor's self esteem.*

Result: If the dentist were to say the same things about his or her own clinical skills, it would sound conceited and self serving. But bragging on the doctor and team to the patient is not only allowed but a must for practice building.

Walter

Prescription #5

The true value of praise was driven home to us at a recent Youth Leadership Forum, our special seminars for high school and college age students. One of the teenagers in the group was abandoned by both of his parents several years before. Here was a boy obviously filled with resentment and anger.

During a seminar exercise, we watched and wondered when he volunteered to come to the front of the group. His classmates then had the chance to say and write down all the attributes about him they appreciated. As the praise came on from his classmates and was written down on a large easel pad in front of the room for all to see, his whole demeanor transformed from "I hate the world" to "Someone really likes me."

Because written praise has a bigger impact than verbal praise, we give every attendee at our dental "Boot Kamps" a pad of fifty "I appreciate _____" notes.

We encourage folks to write these notes to the other

people in the seminar when they say or do something helpful. Because we are creatures of habit, writing down compliments helps people **get into the habit of giving compliments**.
Result: Most people will respond to it as dramatically as our young friend. You cannot only change your own life and that of others, but you can help change the entire environment.

PERSONAL ACTION PLAN

1. Review the list of praiseworthy characteristics you made for each member of your dental team in the Personal Action Plan that follows Chapter 1. Have you succeeded in communicating your praise of their virtues? What else could you add:

Name	*Positive Characteristics*

2. What can you do to heighten morale in the office?

3. Take the pulse of the office. What ways can you think of to improve the treatment of the patients:

4. List three positive things you can say about the dentist to your patients:

_____

_____

_____

5. Since written praise is more potent than verbal praise, what steps will you take to communicate your sincere compliments to your fellow staff members?

_____

_____

_____

Chapter 9

"You have to be tough to work in this dental
office, honey. I decided a long time ago that
I wasn't going to do any extra work until I got
a raise, and so far I've outlasted the doctor
for more than twenty years!"

How to Get a Raise

Imagine this little fantasy.

Eleanor Employee walks into her boss's office.

"You wanted to see me. What can I do for you?" the boss asks.

"On a scale from zero to ten, please tell me how my work performance rates in your eyes."

Her boss doesn't even bat an eye.

"Seven," he says sternly.

"All right," Eleanor replies, not to be denied, "tell me what I must do to raise this seven to a ten."

Linda

Prescription #1

What I like about this hypothetical situation is that the employee's ego is performance-oriented. She's not nervous to talk to the boss and she doesn't waste time. She called the meeting because she wants to know where she stands. She's not afraid to ask. Not content with any number less than ten, she addresses the only real question that matters, "How can I get there from here?"

Eleanor already knows the answer to the question: where do raises come from? That's why her performance is her uppermost concern.

Result: She can only increase her value. In other words, **"Your raise will become effective when you are."**

Prescription #2

People sometimes labor under false assumptions. It would be wise to banish the idea that there's something automatic about a raise.

It's **earned, not expected**.

Criteria should be outlined and team evaluations done on a regular basis. Thus, no one is in the dark about such an important matter.

We've found, in addition, for the team member willing to become his or her own boss, the following breakdown useful regarding a merit increase.

Evaluate yourself in these four areas:

•25% based on your attitude
(cheerful, caring, a joy to work with);
•25% based on your individual evaluation scores
(results match written self and employer evaluations);
•25% based on your sense of responsibility
(willingness to volunteer and harmonize);
•25% based on the health of the practice
(the bottom line financial number the previous year).

Result: You never forget that it's teamwork, cooperation and enthusiasm that builds the practice. Only when the practice is enriched, both net and gross, do salaries get enriched.

Is there a right way and a wrong way to ask for a raise?

Walter
Prescription #3

You bet. Steve Anderson, President of Planned Marketing Associates, refers to my approach as **Grandpa Hailey's Tried and True 4 M (Method for Making More Money) System**.

For purposes of contrast, let's start with the wrong ways first. They're probably more familiar to us anyhow. Consider

two approaches people use all the time. We call them *Somethin'
for Nuthin'* and *Poorhouse Blues*. Instead of celebrating our
contributions, both methods reveal our insecurities.

*"Well, Doctor, I've been working here for twenty years
and I'm ENTITLED to a piece of the increase!"*

This sour grapes sense of entitlement is like a poison
which keeps you expecting and prevents you from achieving.
Result: It sends a guilt message, not a "Hey, I'm effective"
message. And none of us really know how effective we're capable of becoming until we put ourselves on the line.

*"You know, Doctor, the price of everything keeps going
up. With the way I'm living, I'm not sure I can make ends meet
anymore."*

The message here is that though I may not deserve a
raise, I need one anyhow and you ought to take pity on me!
Result: The doctor has to be wondering that if you can't manage your own household, how competent can you be at the job?
How can the team rely on you, much less pay you more?

**Remember that the best way to get a raise—-and to
achieve complete career security—-is to find out what the
dentist doesn't like to do but is doing all the same.**

I'm talking about do-able ideas that you can implement
in the position you already hold without incurring new expens-
es, doing violence to your job description or setting off turf bat-
tles with the dental team. In other words you make life easier
and ultimately make the practice more successful.

Learn how to do that task better than anyone else,
including the dentist. Start taking the responsibility *away* from
the doctor.
Result: You become totally responsible for the outcome of the
task.

In addition, I would make an appointment with the person in charge of results and I would say that it's **my desire to
have more responsibility for outcomes**. Once you have the
go-ahead, ask for permission to return after an appropriate peri-
od of time to give a progress report.

Result: As you accept more responsibility and execute more effectively, you naturally call up that universal law of compensation, "As ye sow. . ." well, you know the rest.

The law of action and reaction is like gravity—it never fails, even if you happen to be working for a tight wad! Like death and taxes, you can depend on it; you just have to give the law a little time to work. Though the idea is many thousand years old, it's as modern today as it was in the time of Socrates or Jesus.

This willingness to do **WIT** (whatever it takes) is the basis for the conversation with the dentist which is **never about a raise but always about responsibility for results**. Essentially, you're helping the team get more of what they want—and less of what they don't want.

Result: You can't fail to be rewarded. You're in the business of advancing the dental team's cause. Pay is just another word for earnings. The one who earns more for the practice gets more from the practice in return.

And should it be necessary to pop the question?

Appeal to the contribution you've made: "You see what I've been producing. Doctor, what else do I need to do to share more in our successes? Are you happy with my results? On a scale from zero to ten, where am I now?"

Result: The person in charge ought to give you a higher number or advise you on what's missing in your performance. If income doesn't increase, it's time for a career change because, if your evaluation is correct, you deserve more money.

PERSONAL ACTION PLAN

1. Rate yourself on a scale of 0 to 10 in these four areas:

       _____ attitude
       _____ contribution to the mission
       _____ willingness to volunteer
       _____ contribution to profitability

2. How can you improve that number in each area?

*attitude:*_____

_____

*contribution to the mission:*_____

_____

*willingness to volunteer:*_____

_____

*contribution to profitability:*_____

_____

3. What things in the office are being neglected or are not being done that you could learn how to do better than anyone else?

_____

_____

_____

4. What are the best ways you can contribute more to the growth of the practice:

_____

_____

Chapter 10

"The doctor learned how to extract teeth many years ago and I'm proud to say that we haven't had to bother messing around with any of this new-fangled perio treatment!"

Continuing to Learn

Graduation Day is called commencement because the student can now *commence* to learn the things necessary to succeed in the field he or she has chosen. In other words, graduation is more a beginning than an end. Only the wise student understands that **you can't get paid for what you know; you get paid only for what you can do.**

To be truly performance-oriented you must become a student of your craft. That involves making a commitment to continue to learn throughout your entire lifetime.

Because things are always changing, staying current suggests that you have the ability to learn, unlearn and relearn. That's the real value of your training. It qualifies you to *run* in the race; it doesn't mean you've already *won* the race.

Consider these facts: the volume of human knowledge is doubling every five to seven years. On the average, each individual will have five careers (not jobs, careers!) over a lifetime.

Walter

Prescription #1

Continuing education is not a luxury; it's a necessity.

There are two kinds of knowledge out there for a dental team member. The first kind, the technical aspects of dentistry, requires you to stay contemporary with what's happening. But

58

that's only fifteen percent of what you need to know.

The other eighty five percent of the knowledge base has not changed since Aristotle, Plato and Ross Perot! That's about relating to people. You've probably noticed—-times change but human nature stays the same.

Learning good human relations and communication skills only has to be done once—-it's your best investment for growth. If downsizing ever occurs, the last one to have to worry is the one creating and serving patients effectively.

So demonstrating a desire to learn is the single smartest activity you can do.

Result: You create the highest inspiration for your team while insuring your own personal success.

Should the team member wait for the dentist to suggest a continuing education program?

Walter

Prescription #2

If you're fortunate enough to work for a dentist who offers educational opportunities, go for it, even if some of it is at your own expense.

Don't forget: you are your own employment agency.

Since your earnings are directly commensurate with your ability to get results, we say: **Know How, Do Now.**

Staying alive means continuing to learn. And grow. And contribute.

Result: It's the best investment you'll ever make—-in yourself and in your future.

Linda

Prescription #3

Dentists are the best white collar employers. More than almost any other profession, they are committed as a group to continuing education for themselves and their teams.

School is never out for the professional.

Opportunities in dentistry are a well kept secret. An attitude of gratitude should accompany any chance to learn more than you're given. Knowledge is one of the few things no one can take from you, one of the few things you take with you wherever you go.

One thing that distinguishes dentistry in the general field of health is the excellent range of seminars available in the clinical, management and people aspects of a practice. From what I've seen over the last twenty years, there's nothing like an informed dental team.

Practices that learn together, stay together.

In 1985, seven years after I started consulting and speaking on dental practice management, I realized that one day seminars are great. So two and three day workshops in a smaller group setting would be a plus for dentists and their teams.

Two Day Conferences by the Bay began in 1985 and continue to attract dental teams from across the United States and Canada. Offices report magnificent changes in running the front desk, chairside communication, practice building, and most of all, highly skilled teams.

When respect is high and skills are shared, the jealousy that arises when people of different pay scales work together is eliminated very quickly.

Result: Lowering the barriers to learning encourages every member of the team to advance their knowledge and certification. People "burn out" from jealousy and disrespect, not from hygiene, assisting or dental business duties.

What about dental environments that do not encourage advancement?

Walter

Prescription #4

You may not have access to the many seminars and conferences and national meetings, but there are audio tapes of those seminars! Instead of playing the radio on the way to work, pop in a tape.

Your education is your personal responsibility.

There's no reason not to learn every day. If the dental office does not have a library, a public library will do. Your library has a national hook-up and can get you any book you want. Ask your dentist to assign you books to be read. Having a team member teach at the morning huddle or the weekly meeting the information he or she learns is a great idea.

The best way to learn something is to teach it. Like the old Romans said, Quo dice, quo ducet (The one who teaches, learns).

Result: People like to work where they grow and expand their minds.

PERSONAL ACTION PLAN

1. Create your own continuing education program. List all the things that you would most like to learn:

_____

_____

_____

_____

_____

_____

2. Where can you find the information you've listed above?

_____

_____

_____

_____

_____

3. Write down your daily schedule:

_____

_____

_____

_____

_____

_____

_____

_____

_____

_____

_____

Review the list you made in #1. At what time of day will you spend your half hour of self study?

Chapter 11

**"Hey, I've got it! If we just don't ask our patients
to have treatment done, we won't have to worry
about why they always say 'no' anymore!"**

Developing ESP
(Everybody Search Plan)

The hardest person to do without is the person who brings in the business.

This is one area where every team member can increase his or her value to the practice. The selling of dentistry need not be the exclusive domain of the dentist. In the same way that everyone on the team is responsible for the comfort and health of the patient, everyone on the team is equally responsible for creating new patients.

Remember that the only purpose of the practice is to create happy, paying patients.

Walter

Prescription #1
On the job:

Ask and it shall be given;
Seek and you shall find;
Knock and it shall be opened.
THE KEY is in the **ASKing**.

Take responsibility to **ask every patient who comes into the office if the members of his or her family have a happy dental home.**

Invite patients to bring their friends into the office. Let them see for themselves the quality of care and the environment of dental health that your team creates.

Result: People respond to genuine enthusiasm. We call it BLT—believability, likability and trust. This generates sincere respect for the team and for the practice.

Prescription #2
Off the job:

On average each individual has about 250 people in his or her **arc of influence**. Whether new neighbors or old, relations or in-laws, friends or associates, vendors or merchants you deal with, this is a group of people you're likely to talk to about almost anything—a new film or a new fashion, a change in the weather or a change in the White House. **If it has common impact it will cause you to discuss it.**

Enter the subject of dentistry. The odds are one in two that people in your arc of 250 have no happy dental home. Here's a chance to recommend your team.
Result: Because you're informing them of professional excellence, they are not under any obligation to buy anything. Instead people are pleased you took the time to let them know. **Keeping it simple helps.**

Prescription #3

The subject of the team bringing in more business is an excellent topic for a team planning session. Some practices will favor wanting more quality patients while other practices may prefer to focus on getting patients of record to respond to full comprehensive dentistry.

In any case, **involving everyone on board in a Goal Action Plan for the expansion of the practice is a win-win situation.** Although ideas may be "a dime a dozen," they become sparkling gems when put into action.

The value of an ESP brainstorming session is that everyone gets a chance to give input. Sometimes what may seem like a minor remark, one that will seem obvious later on but at present is simply overlooked, can make a major difference.

It should be noted that some of the best strategies in selling and marketing have been invented by the players who are on line day in and day out. You know better than anyone else what people are looking for in dental health care. And no one is more qualified to sell the quality of dental health care that you and your team actually provide to patients. Looking at your job with your eye on enriching business can prove to be a valuable asset.

Result: Encouraging everyone to come up with suggestions helps create that vital degree of camaraderie that spells **TEAM:** *Together Everyone Achieves More.*

It also helps erase that artificial line between *selling* dentistry and *doing* dentistry.

Linda
Prescription #4

Setting a goal of each team member bringing one new patient to the practice a week can really boost business.

Get business cards made with your name, function and the dental office's address and phone number on it. Every time you interact with the outside world—-whether at church, the dry cleaners, or even a restaurant—-drop off a card.

"I work for the finest dentist in town. Please call me and we'll arrange a convenient time for you to meet us."

Moreover, get in the habit of **collecting other people's business cards.** Start your own network.

Result: It's been my experience that team members who constantly and conscientiously recruit new patients enjoy a greater degree of emotional and financial security.

PERSONAL ACTION PLAN

1. Ask ten people a day if they have a happy dental home and who they know that needs one.

2. Ask the practice administrator or dentist what the plan is for attracting new, quality patients. In what ways can you implement or vitalize this plan?

Chapter 12

"Why should we stick our necks out?
I think we should keep the office door
locked from now on so we don't ever
have anything screw up anymore!

Going Above and Beyond the Call of Duty

As the last chapter—-indeed the whole booklet of pre-scriptions—-implies, **it is impossible to help another without helping yourself.**

Thinkers from a variety of backgrounds, from religious prophets to giants of industry, have called this insight with different names: The Law of Cause and Effect, the Golden Rule, the Principle of Action and Reaction, the Law of Karma or Universal Compensation. However you say it, it spells this truth: There is a universal balancing act going on.

Walter

Prescription #1

If you help enough other people get more of what they want and less of what they don't want, you'll never have to worry about what you want.

Rather than fill yourself with the anxiety that comes from trying to measure your worth in every situation, knowing that what you sow is what you'll reap allows you to relax and focus on the life you want to create.

Result: You stop living your life in order to satisfy the unrealistic expectations of others, so many of whom are not living any more!

We call it the freedom to go above and beyond the call of duty.

This willingness to walk the extra mile may seem, to the cynic in all of us, a colossal error, doomed to failure, the sure road of a sucker.

That defensive, intimidated, skeptical voice in us asks, Why would I ever do more than I have to do?

Walter

Prescription #2
In order to:
- escape the mental prison of skepticism itself!
- overcome the fear that keeps us intimidated.
- open the way for a generosity of spirit.
- develop personal initiative and self reliance.
- become one with courage.
- make yourself indispensable.
- protect you from a loss of employment.
- insure the choicest of jobs.
- aid in the building of a keener imagination.
- discover new and better ways of providing service.
- enjoy the pleasure of being purposeful.
- defeat aimlessness and procrastination.
- build self-mastery.
- create the habit of a positive mental attitude.

Do more than you're paid to do! It's the only way to get paid more for what you do.

You're setting the table for a marvelous banquet.
Result: You become all that you can be.

The greatest benefit does not come to the one for whom the service is rendered; it comes to the one who renders the service.

Linda

Prescription #3
Expressions of care can have compelling results.

In one of the most successful offices I've ever had the pleasure of consulting with, at the end of November a team member gathers the names of all the patients who lost a family member over the last twelve months. During the first week of December the dental practice sends poinsettias to each of the families with a note, *Thinking of you during this holiday season.*

Another thoughtful dental practice makes sure that, first thing in the morning, each member of the team circles the name of a patient on yesterday's calendar. Before lunch time, each team member writes a personal note to that patient.

A third practice makes sure that they offer, after treatment, to send the patient home in a cab, particularly if he or she has had major dentistry performed.

But doing the little things for the patient is only half of the story.

We all know it's easy to look busy. But when we have a few minutes between appointments, it's nice to say to a team member, "I have ten minutes. What can I do for you?"
Result: Having risen above the call of duty, we invoke another level of relatedness.

Ask yourself, "Do I have my priorities in place?"
Number one is the patient; number two is the practice; number three is the doctor and the total team.

This way it always comes out right.

Walter

Prescription #4
A final thought. The Law of Compensation also works in reverse. That's why we caution: **Never put yourself in a situation where you're getting paid more than you're worth.**

If you allow your salary to exceed your contribution, you'll pay for it somewhere down the line. To keep the law working on our side, the method to getting is giving, and the way to become a member of a great team is:

Always do what you ought to do when you ought to do it, whether you want to or not—-NO DEBATE.

PERSONAL ACTION PLAN

1. What can you do immediately to give more and do more than you're paid to do:

_____

_____

_____

_____

2. Who in the practice needs your help the most?

_____

_____

_____

3. How can you help them?

_____

_____

_____

4. What can you do for your patients that is unexpected and kind?

_____

_____

Linda and Walter's
Daily Set of Twelve Reminders:

1. Take all gossip back to its source.

2. Check all personal baggage at the door.

3. Become a fixer, not a finger pointer.

4. Know your role on the team at all times.

5. Support the dentist and spouse as co-owners of the practice.

6. Whenever possible, take the pressure off the dentist.

7. Make your appearance match your patient's expectations.

8. Praise your team and your doctor.

9. Always seek to increase your value to the practice.

10. Be a constant learner.

11. Create more happy, paying patients.

12. Do more than you're paid to do.

Epilogue

We have been in the business of helping dental teams enjoy greater financial and emotional security for some time, but we are always learning more.

We welcome your feedback.

Your responses and anecdotes, examples and ideas not only mean a lot to us personally but for making future editions of our handbook more valuable to the dental community at large. We're easy to reach:

Linda Miles
Miles & Associates
484 Viking Drive, Suite 190
Virginia Beach, VA 23452
804-498-0014
fax 804-498-0290
toll free 800-922-0866

Walter Hailey
Planned Marketing Associates
P.O. Box 345
Hunt, TX 78024
210-238-4357
fax 210-238-4075
toll free 800-HUNT-TEX
or
800-BOOTKAMP

Linda Miles

A partial list of mentors who have helped in so many areas of my life:

Don
Mother
Dad
Grandfather & Grandmother Lance
Grandfather & Grandmother Estep
Brother, Ted
Sisters, Pat and Bobbie
Daughter, LaDona
Son, David
Son-in-Law, Lee Young
Louise Thacker
Bailey Ann Mills
David and Naomi Richardson
D. W. McCormick
Lucille Kirk
Myrtle Ratcliff Butt
Granny Miles
Mary Ellen Paulo
Dr. Jim Nelson
Dr. Stephen Morrow
Dr. Jan Lockman
Dr. Jim Lance
Dr. Richard S. Wilson
Dr. Omer Reed
Ann Ehrlich
Dr. Neal Brahe
Dr. Paul Jacobi
Ken Olsen
Dr. Louis Beall
Dr. Tom McDougal
Dr. Charles Wood
Dr. Joel Safer
Dr. Jonathan Bregman
Dr. Denny Mills
Robert Henry
Ralph Hood
Bobbie Gee
Zig Ziglar
Michael Aun
Rosit Perez
Leslie Charles
Cavett Robert
Mark Victor Hanson
Jim tunney
Dr. Howard Grand
Dr. Pete Jenson
Dr. Jack Mullen
L. D. Pankey

Dr. Marquita Poynter
Bonnie Sue Davis
Dr. Burt Press
Dr. Arlen Lackey
Reta Barnes Hill
Brian Tracy
Joy Millis
Ruth and George Port
Sally Snyder
Lee Tarvin
Mary Arnold
Carol George
Lisa Baxter
Michelle McGinnis
Leslie Daughety
Connie Taylor
Regina Thomann
Char Sweeney
Pat Gore
Cindy Ishimoto
Diane Meisenberg
Dr. Tom Hughes
Sandy Pickering
Dr. Andy Doerfler
Dr. Gary Fox
Dr. Herb Land
Walter Hailey
Dr. Jerry Hayes
Dick Hale
Dr. Jim Bramson
Pat Rice
Marion and Wolf Bolz
Dr. Charles Ray
Louise Ropog
Dr. Richard Sullivan, Jr.
Virginia Sullivan Stokes
Mary McCutcheon
Betty Bartley
Dr. Janie Soxman
Janie Moorer
Lee Shelton
Dr. Larry Pearson
Dr. Charles Barker
Dr. Jim Vollmer
Dr. J. Klooster
Dr. Carole Pratt

Walter Hailey

Dental Mentors:

Harry Albers
Chuck Alexander
Moody Alexander
Wick & Jana Alexander
Don Allen
Andy Anderson
Billy Anderson
Ernie & Karen Anderson
Donald E. Arens
Carol J. Austin
Victor & Kim Avis
Ronald & Nancy Avis
Ronald & Diane Ayala
Stanley & Elaine Barbakoff
Jay Barnett
Sheard & Debbie Ber
Ray Bertolotti
Pat & Lani Beug
Geoffrey Bild
Joseph Blaes
Cliff & Judi Blumberg
Paul Bonner
Les Bortel
Ronald & Sally Boscher
Rich & Jan Boyes
Alan Broadbent
Dana Brockington
John & Bonnie Buist
Raul Caffesse
Douglas Campbell
Joe Campbell & Emliy Ley
Tom Carns
Dan & Leslie Cassidy
James Cassidy
Gordon Christensen
Bill & Eileen Cohen
Brad Coleman
Kevin Cooke
Bob Cowie
Larry Daugherty
Daniel & Cathy Davis
Sam & Carol Davis
Peter Dawson

Marianne Day & Grant Watson
Guy Deyton
Bill Dickerson
Don DiGiulian
Hugh Doherty
John R. Droter
John Droter
Jim and Suzanne Du Molin
James & Vanessa Fey
Gary & Patrice Fishbein
Hugh Flax
Terry Fohey
Bennett Fontenot
Alan Fryday
Leslie Fullerton
Vijay & Kirthi Garach
Naresh & Vicky Garach
Samili Garach
David & Cindy Garber
Michael Garber
Tom George
Steve & Debra Glassman
Corey Gold
Erwin & Celia Gold
Ray Gold
Alan Goldstein
Cary Goldstein
Ron Goldstein
Josh Green
Jim Gorgol
Cal & Lynn Gray
Jeff Gray
Josh Green
Earl Gunn Jr.
Mark D. Hackbarth
Bob Hamrick
Eric Hamrick
Steve Hamrick
Kathy Hays
Dave Heller
Dan Hinckley
Don Hill
Richard Hixson

Jerry Hoffman
Larry Hoffmann
Sarah Hopkins
Joleen Jackson
Michel Jahjah
Glenn Johnson
Kevin and Kerry Johnson
Lloyd Johnston
Adrian Jurim
Erla Kay
Marianne Kehoe
Bill Keller
Ron Keller
Tom Keller
Kal Khaled
Ralph & Mona Kimbrough
Bill & Jan King
Gary & Genny Klugman
Georf Knight
John Kois
Phil Korpi
Dan & Donna Laizure
Estel & Arlen Landreth
Buddy Lee
Imtiaz Manji
McHenry (Mac) Lee
Mark Link
Bill & Jeanne Locante
Stephen & Betty Marks
Tom McAndrews
Craig McClure
Tom McDougal
Sally & Chuck McKenzie
Ed & Virginia Mendlik
Bob Menzel
Leon Merrick
Gary Michels
Linda and Don Miles
Travis McFee
Fred Monti
Chris Moody
Mike Morgan
Ted Morgan
Jim & Vicki Morrish
Geraldine Morrow
Gerry Mundy
Dave Nakanishi
Guy Nash

Woody Oakes
Mike and Patrice O'Brien
Harvey Passes
Larry & Sari Pearson
Fred Peck
Keith & Kim Phillips
Jorge Pinero
Risa Pollack
Ruth Port
Fred Polzin
Ron & Judy Presswood
Jim Pride
Ron Presswood
Ralph Reilly
Pete & Linda Roach
Howard Rochestie
Ike Rolader
Larry Rosenthal
Lloyd Rothschild
John A. Sanders
Chris Sager
Ken Schmitt
Steve Schwartz
Gene Seidner
Joe Shea
Fred & Lois Shockley
Steve Sorensen
Jim and Kathy Sparaga
Pam Strother
William Strupp
Charlie Stuart
David Sturgeon
Randy Talaski
Tom Volck
Glenn Weisel
Ben White
Ron & Bunny Wickum
Witt & Pat Wilkerson
Larry & Dottie Williams
Clark & Susan Williams
Michael Wise
Thomas & Pat Worcester
Rick Workman
Bob & Patricia Zampieri
Greg & Pamela Zollo
And all of our Dental Boot Kamp
and Graduate Boot Kamp Alumni
Academy of Laser Dentistry

American Dental Association
American Academy of Dental
   Practice Administration
American Academy of
Periodontology
Canadian Dental Association
Chicago Midwinter Dental Meeting
Dental Resource Alliance
Federation Dental International
Greater New York Dental Meeting
Hinman Dental Meeting
Journe Dental
Minnasota Dental Association
New Orlean Dental Association
Pankey Class 1+++
Profitabl Dentist
Texas Dental Association
Yankee Dental Meeting